The Complete Quilling Handbook

by Pat Green

Reprinted 1986, 1987, 1988, 1989

ISBN 0 9513853 0 5

Published by
Pat Green, Past Times, Cumberhills Road, Duffield, Derby DE6 4HA

Printed by
J. H. Hall & Sons Limited, Siddals Road, Derby DE1 2PZ

Contents

Introduction

During the past six years I have been fortunate enough to have participated in the 20th Century revival of the ancient craft of quilling or paper filigree.

I am delighted therefore to have been given the opportunity to share with you the skills and pleasures of this rewarding pastime.

A Brief History

The first records of quilling are in the histories of the earliest civilisations around the Mediterranean sea.

Narrow strips of papyrus were rolled into coils and scrolls, gilded and then burnished to imitate precious gold and silver filigree.

15th Century records show that the poorer religious bodies in this country were using gilded paper in much the same way and by the 17th Century "picture ornaments" were beginning to appear in people's homes. (See illustration, page 19).

Designs up to this time were formal. Gilding of the cream or ivory paper was popular but little colour was used, interest being added by the use of small shells or beads.

Of special note was the heraldic work, which, with its bold use of colour and gilding, was very impressive.

An 18th Century revival increased still further the uses made of quilling in the home and it became a recognised craft for the young ladies to learn. The Teaching of quilling became a profession, and patterns were printed in the ladies magazines of the period.

With the resources available to-day the only restriction in designs is in the limit of our imagination.

Basic skills are easily mastered, and you will soon find yourself able to produce mobiles, miniatures, jewellery and greetings cards to delight yourself and your friends.

Happy Quilling

Pat Green

Basic Tools, Materials and Equipment

Papers

Widths — 2mm
3mm
5mm
10mm

Lengths — normally 450mm which may be torn by hand into the required length.

Glue

A clear drying non-elastic paper glue.

Work Surface

A piece of fibre board or polystyrene is ideal for a work base. Patterns etc. may then be pinned onto this, over which greaseproof or plastic will give a suitable work surface.
When the quilled shapes are glued to each other, any glue seeping between the shapes is easily removed from these surfaces.

Tools

Below are illustrated quilling tools which are available.
(It is also possible to make a tool for yourself by sawing off the tip of the eye of a sewing needle. Be very careful however as this could be extremely dangerous, particularly in childrens' hands).

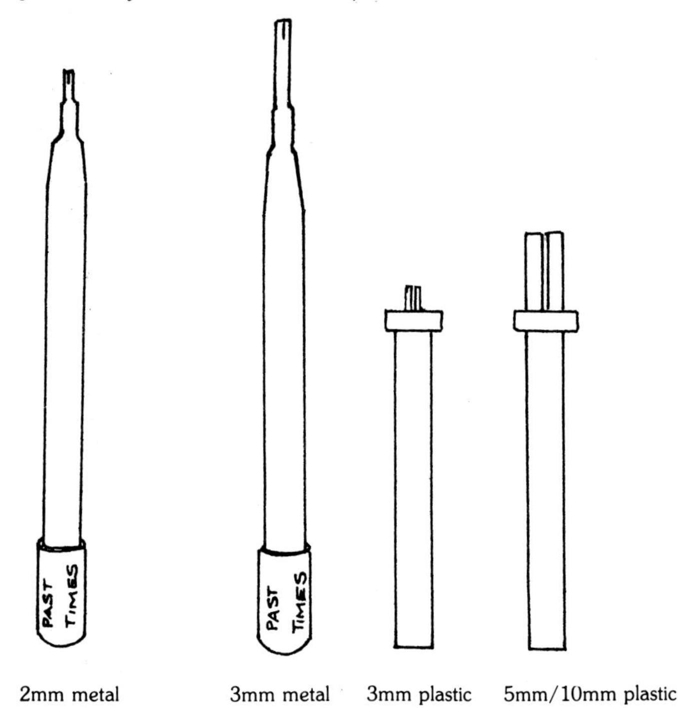

2mm metal | 3mm metal | 3mm plastic | 5mm/10mm plastic

Measure

0 | 37½mm | 75mm | 150mm

Rolling the papers

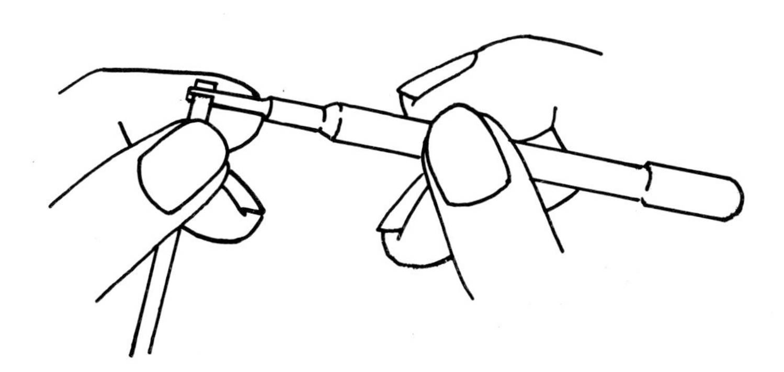

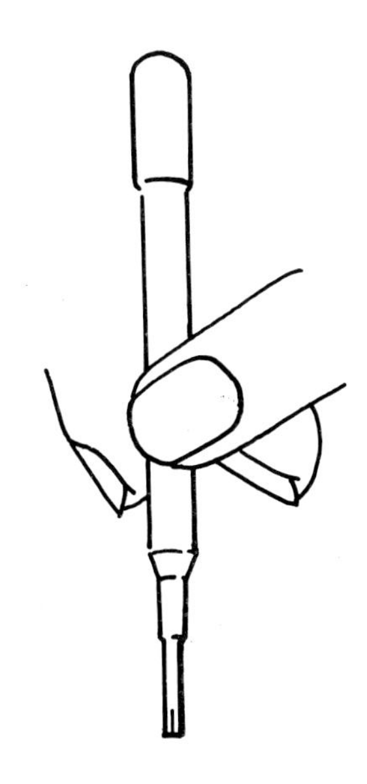

1. Put the tip of the paper into the slot in the quilling tool and roll it into a tight coil, turning the tool either towards or away from you.

   At this stage, the tension of your quilling is determined. If the coil is too loose, give a few additional turns on the tool. If the coil is too tight, loosen the grip you have on the paper when it is rolled.

2. Allow the coil to fall freely from the tool, forcefully removing the coil will distort it.

Making the Mosaic Shapes

All the mosaic shapes are made from the closed mosaic coil

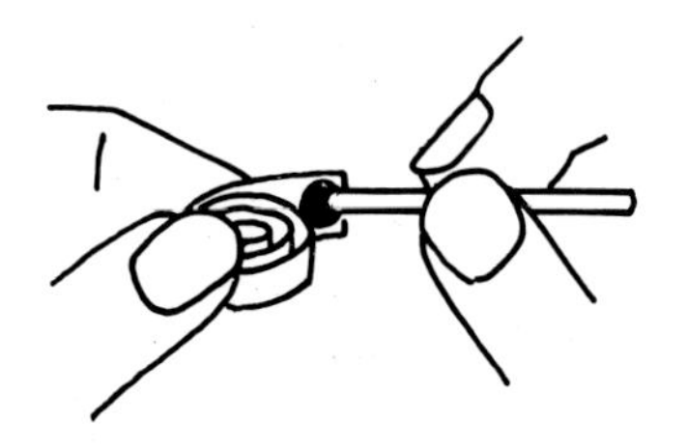

1. **Mosaic Coil**
   Glue down the tip of the rolled coil

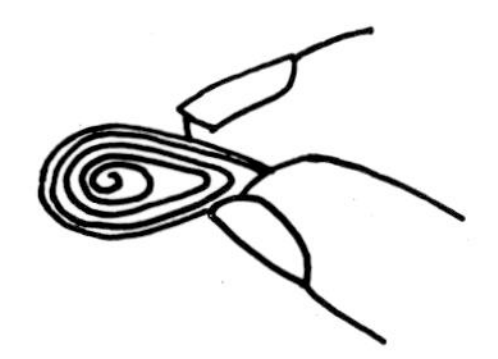

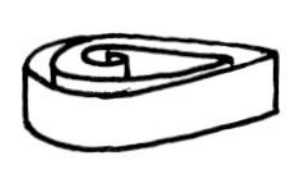

2. **Eye Shape**
   Pinch the mosaic coil to a point at one end

3. **Drop Shape**
   Repeat No. 2, moving the centre of the coil to the end being pinched

4. **Petal Shape**
   Repeat No. 2, then slightly curve the pinched end

5. **Diamond Shape**
   Pinch the mosaic coil to points at both ends

6. **Leaf Shape**
   Repeat No. 5, slightly curving the points in opposite directions

7. **Oval Shape**
   Slightly squash the mosaic coil

8. **Square Shape**
Press the mosaic coil into shape with fingers and thumbs of both hands

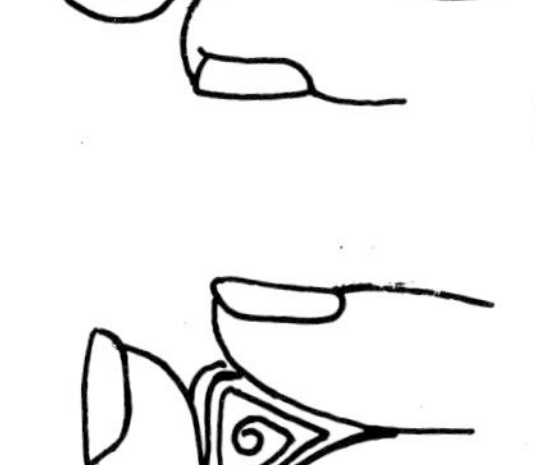

9. **Rectangle Shape**
Repeat No. 8, slightly lengthening two opposite sides

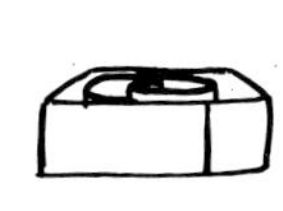

10. **Triangle Shape**
Press the mosaic coil into shape with the finger and thumb of one hand against the finger of the other

11. **Star Shape**
Pinch points at both ends of the mosaic coil, then push the fingers and thumbs towards each other forming the other points

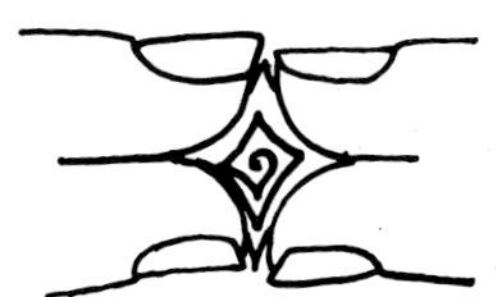

12. **Half Moon Shape**
Curve the mosaic coil round the largest part of the quilling tool

13. **Shield Shape**
Pinch a point at one end of the mosaic coil, then repeat No. 12

14. **Tulip Shape**
Pinch points at both ends of the mosaic coil, then push the fingers together to form the centre point

Making the Filigree Shapes

All the filigree shapes are made from the open filigree coil

1. **Filigree Coil**

2. **Scroll Shape**
   Roll filigree coils towards each other from both ends

3. **'S' Shape**
   Roll filigree coils away from each other at both ends

4. **Heart Shape**
   Fold the paper in half and roll filigree coils towards each other from both ends

5. **'V' Shape**
   Fold the paper in half and roll filigree coils away from each other at both ends

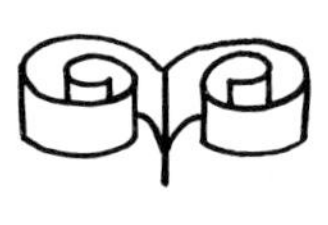

6. **Feelers Shape**
   Repeat No. 5, then glue the sides of the 'V' shape together

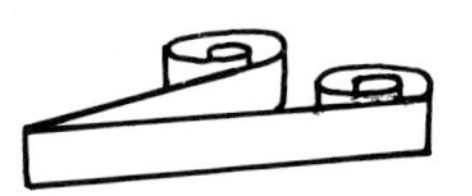

7. **Quotes Shape**
   Fold the paper in half and roll filigree coils in the same direction at both ends

8. **'P' Shape**

Fold the paper in half and roll the two ends together into a filigree coil

9. **Arrowhead Shape**

Fold the paper in half, then fold the two ends into the middle of the 'V' securing in the centre with a little glue. Roll the two folded ends into filigree coils, towards the centre

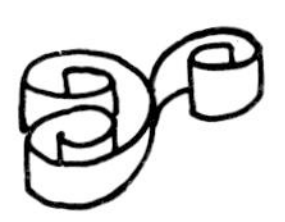

10. **Three-coil Shapes**

Fold the paper in half, then roll the two ends and the fold into three filigree coils

11. **Stretched Shapes**

Take any of the filigree shapes, place the tip of the tool inside the coil to be stretched and carefully pull open the coil

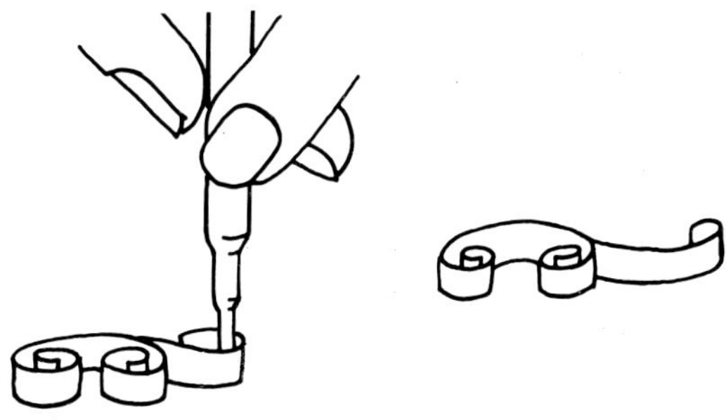

12. **Spiral**

Roll the paper at an angle round a knitting needle, cocktail stick, or other such item

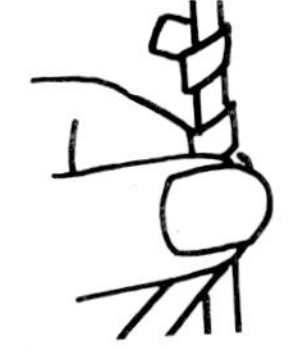

13. **The Peg**

Glue down the tip of the paper before removing the tight coil carefully from the tool

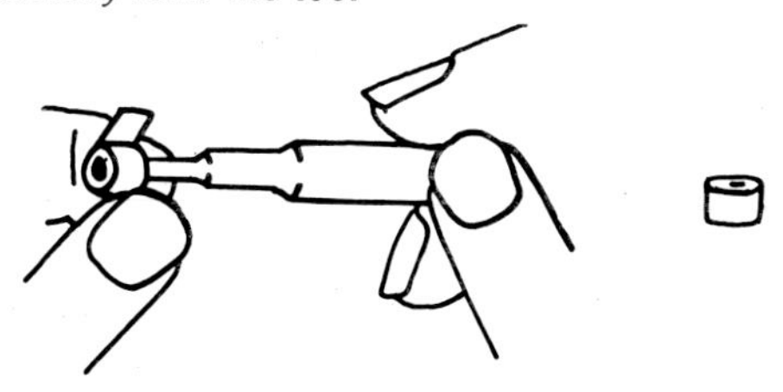

Special Shapes

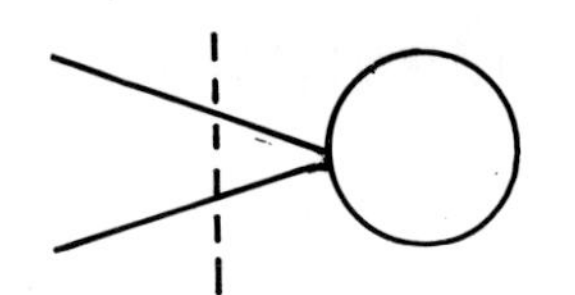
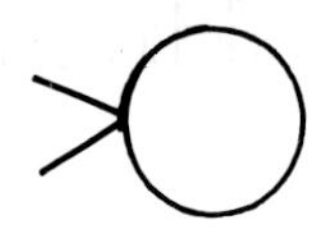

1. When adding folded papers to a design for beaks, legs etc., always use a larger paper than is necessary and trim to size when the glue is dry.

2. Peg shapes may be stuck inside coils for eyes etc.

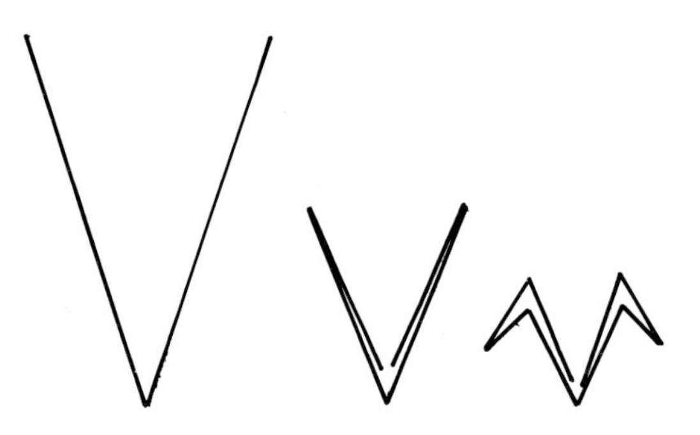

3. Blades of grass, corn or leaves are made by folding a strip of paper in half and then half again, securing the tips with glue. A further fold then gives the grass effect.

4. Two-coloured shapes may be made by either rolling two different strips together side by side, or sticking one paper onto the end of another. These two coloured shapes are most effective for butterflies, fish, flowers etc.

5. Cones are made from peg shapes, their centres being pushed upwards by a pencil or other cone shaped object.

Making up Designs

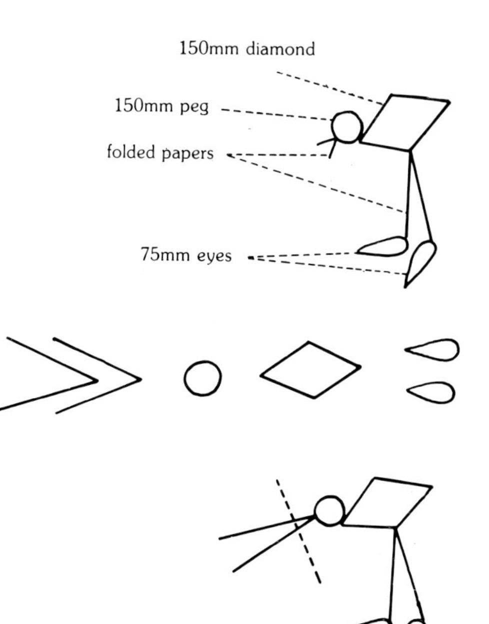

1. Cover the selected pattern with either greaseproof paper or plastic and use this as your working surface.

2. Make the required shapes.

3. Assemble the shapes, glue them to each other and leave to dry.

4. Trim off any papers not required.

5. If the design is to be attached to another surface, place dabs of glue all over the reverse of the quilling and position where required.

6. By altering the position of the shapes, designs may be further animated as illustrated below.

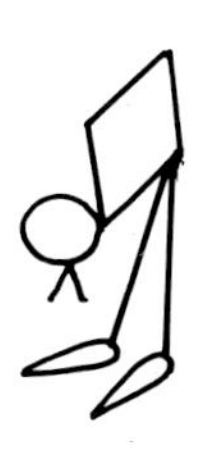

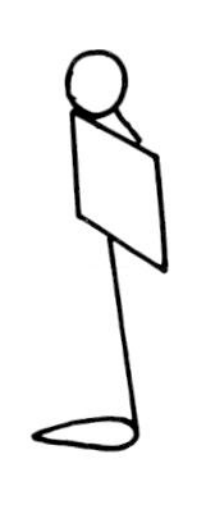

Size Variation in Quilling

Scale:
2mm tool
2mm paper,
75mm long

Scale:
3mm tool
3mm paper,
150mm long

These birds illustrate just four of the many size variations possible using different tools and paper lengths.

This is particularly useful when creating parent and baby animals, necklace and earring sets etc.

Scale:
5mm/10mm tool
5mm paper, 300mm long

Scale:
5mm/10mm tool
10mm paper, 450mm long

Dimension in Quilling

1. Bases

Bases made up from mosaic coils in papers of different widths make ideal stands for quilled animals, plants etc.

2. Furniture

Dolls house furniture may be created using cocktail sticks covered with peg shapes for legs and stands. Pegs are incorporated in the design of the table top or chair seat through which the cocktail stick is threaded. The stick is then cut to size and hidden by further pegs, usually of 10mm width paper.

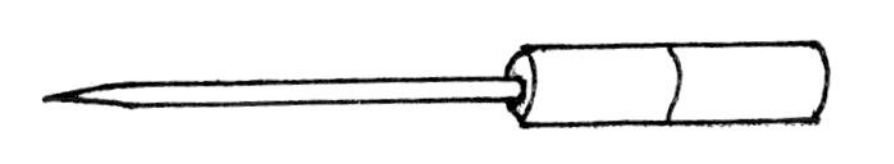

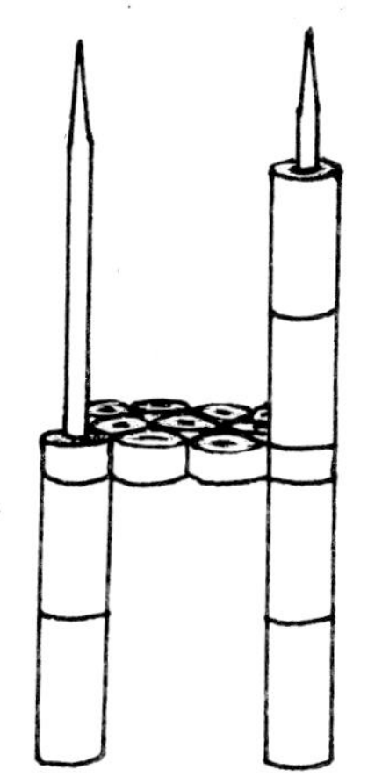

e.g. Table and chair, inside front cover.
Bird table, inside back cover.

3. Three Dimensional Designs

A third dimension may be given by sticking extra shapes on to an existing two dimensional design.

e.g. Christmas Tree (inside back cover)

4. Mobiles

Either two or three dimensional designs are very attractive when hung either alone or in groups as mobiles, they move very well in the slightest breeze.
The 5mm or 10mm papers are better because of their additional weight.

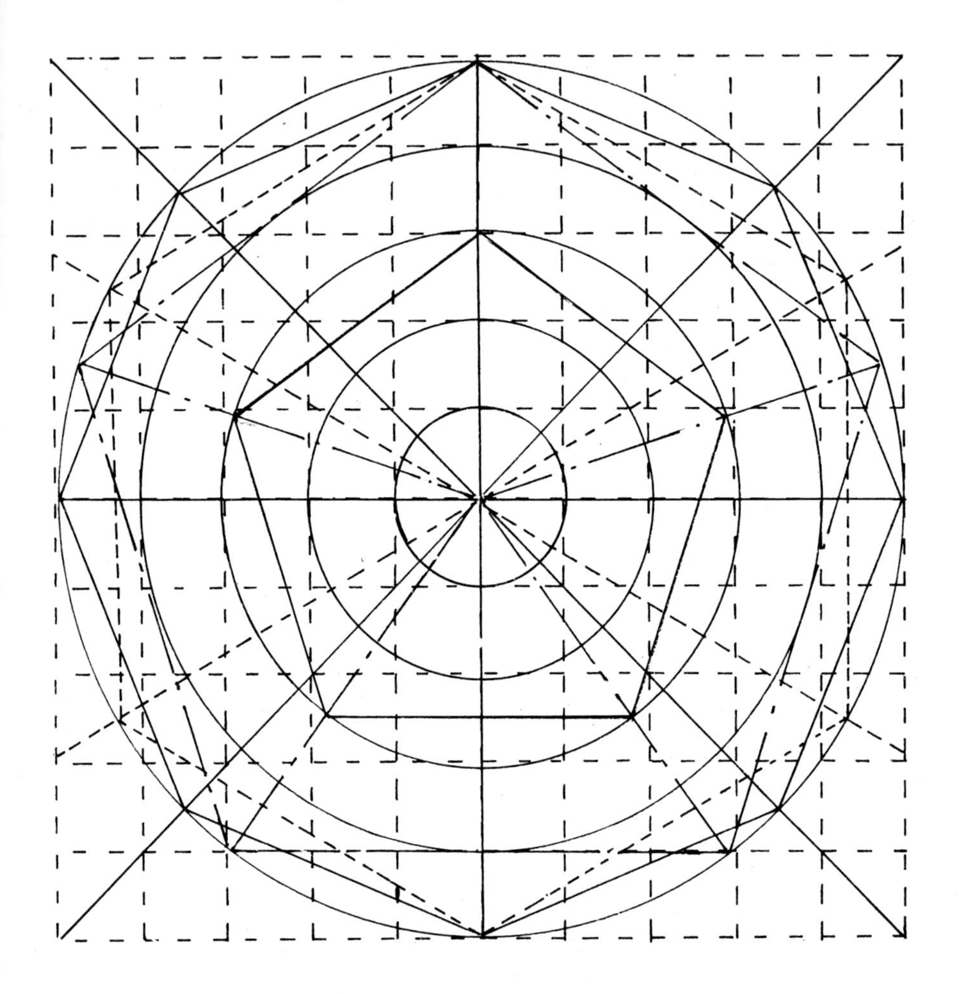

Quilling Geometric Designs Using a grid

Key

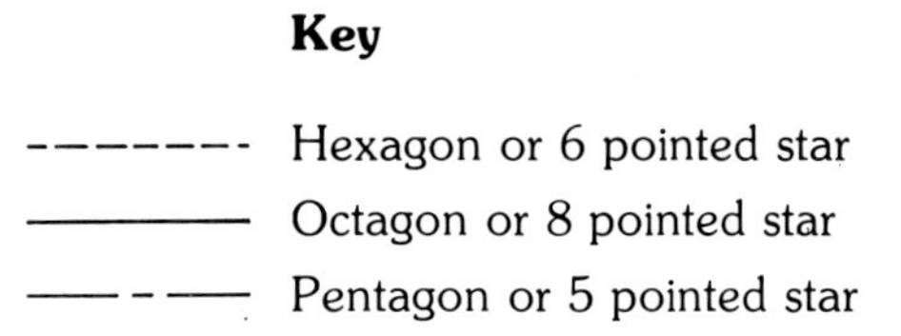

A grid is always a useful quilling aid to have. Guide lines may be used for any geometric design, not only those mentioned in the above key, but also squares, rectangles, circles, crosses etc.

Outlining

If your geometric design is to be enclosed, first complete the filling-in shapes and glue them together, then take the enclosing paper or papers and wrap them round the shapes sticking in place as you do so.

Embellishment

Quilling has been embellished throughout the course of history in various ways, adding colour, glitter and interest to the completed works of art. In the past small beads, seed pearls, mica and metallic threads were used, below are ideas for you to try.

1. Beads, seed pearls, sequins, glitter etc., may all be stuck on to the quilled designs and used for pictures, greetings cards, Christmas decorations, mobiles etc.
2. Background materials have a great influence on pictures. Experiment for yourself with metallic board, different fabrics and textured papers.
3. Gilding, an embellishment very much associated with ancient rolled paper work, may be achieved in various ways without the use of very expensive gold or silver leaf:-

   (a) Pour a little gold, silver or coloured water paint onto a sheet of glass or mirror, spread it on the surface, then place your completed design on the paint so that only the cut edges are coloured.

   (b) Begin similarly to (a), use a small roller and roll the water paint onto the finished design.

   (c) Gold or silver polish normally used for refurbishing picture frames can be wiped onto the design with a piece of cloth or your finger, and then polished with a clean duster.
4. Aerosol paint sprays may be used for three different purposes:-

   (a) Either completely cover the quilled design, or colour selected areas.

   (b) To create a pattern on a backing sheet by spraying through a quilled design.

   (c) To give a print by using the quilled design when it is still wet.

Templates

The templates on these two pages may be used in many ways, some ideas are as follows:-

a. Completely fill in the outline with quilled shapes, e.g. no. 5, the bell.

b. Frame the outline with quilled shapes, e.g. no. 2, the flower.

c. Fill in the outline with a lattice of papers, e.g. no.1, the valentine.

d. Make into small decorated cards for gift cards etc., e.g. no. 7, the christmas tree.

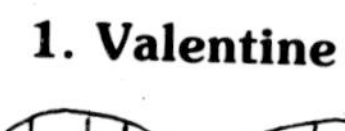

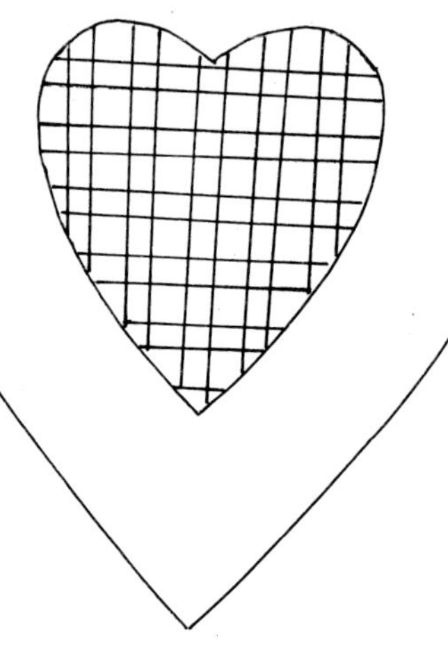

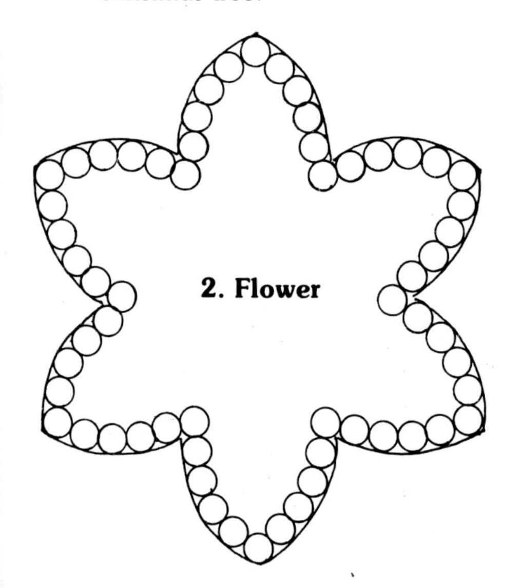

e. Use as a backing or a base for a quilled design, see back cover.

f. Individual mobiles for hanging on Christmas Trees etc.

g. Group mobile, see page 37.

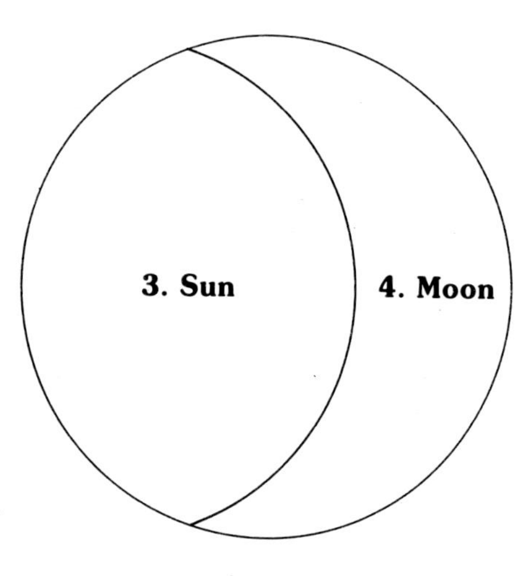

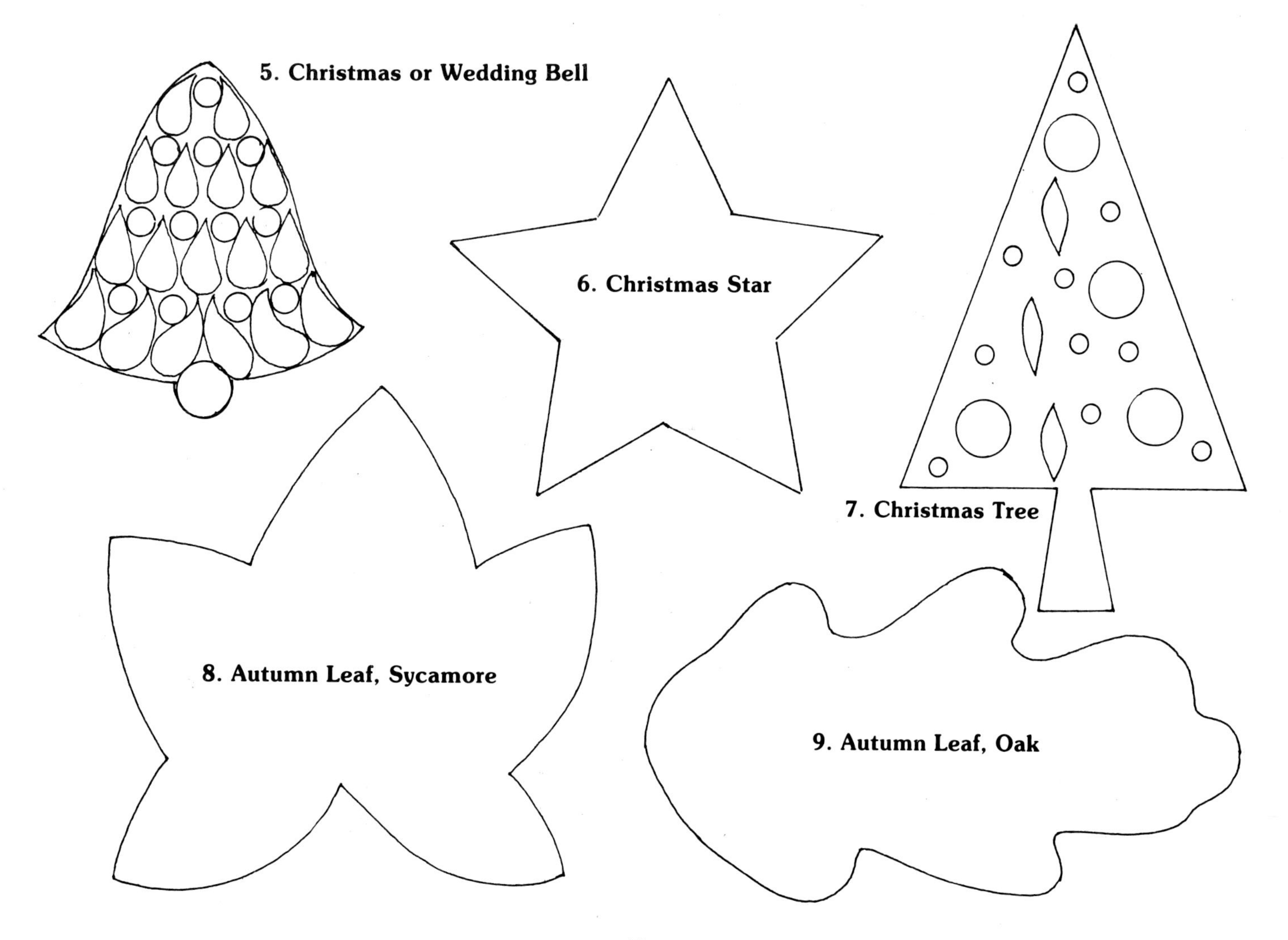
5. Christmas or Wedding Bell
6. Christmas Star
7. Christmas Tree
8. Autumn Leaf, Sycamore
9. Autumn Leaf, Oak

Curved Surface Decoration

When decorating eggs, spheres or any curved surface with quilling, the shapes are glued one at a time onto the surface.

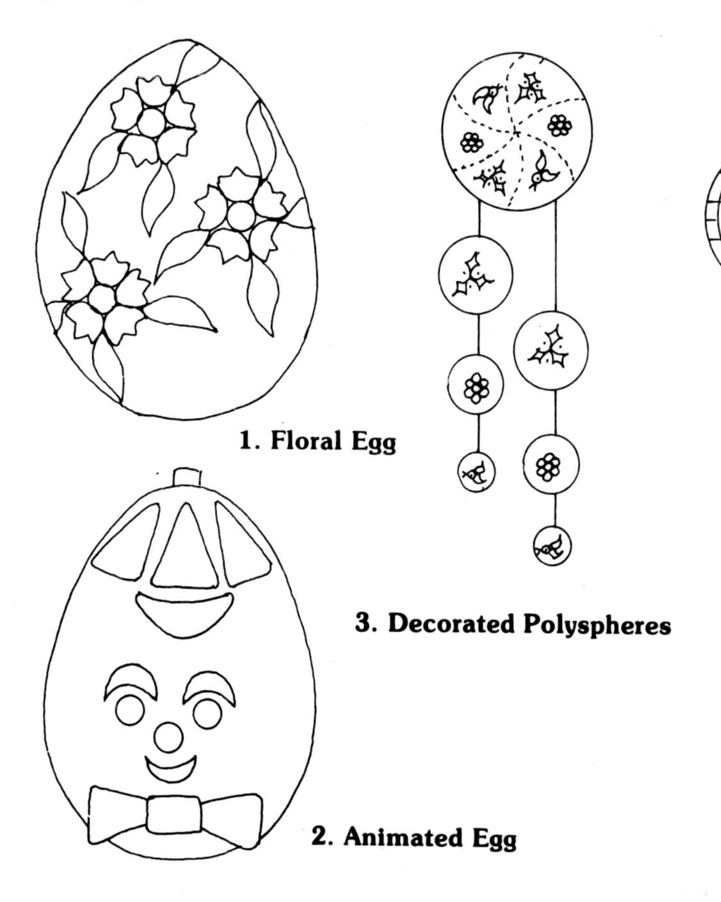

1. Floral Egg

2. Animated Egg

3. Decorated Polyspheres

4. Three dimensional eggs or spheres

Three dimensional spheres or eggs may be made by using an egg or polysphere as a mould.
The quilled egg or sphere is made in two separate halves which are glued together.

a. Make a grid round the shape by sticking papers to each other.

b. Stick the quilled shapes onto the grid, keeping the two halves separate.

c. Cut the grid papers where the halves meet, and remove them from the mould.

d. Stick together the two halves

5. Curved Shapes

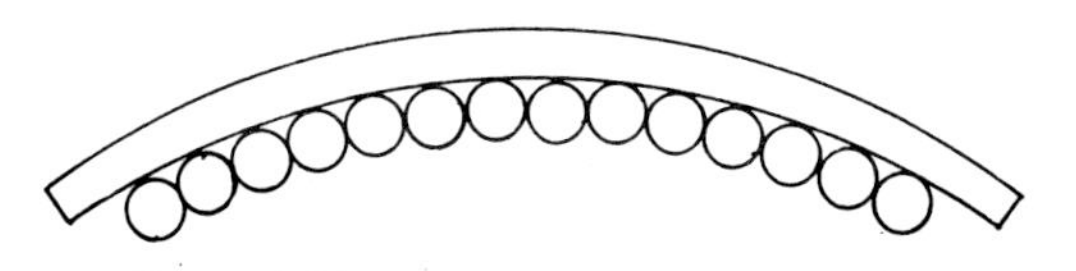

Curved Shapes may be made by using a mould such as a saucer or wineglass and building up your design on the curve, sticking the shapes to each other.
The umbrella on page 27 was made this way.

PAT

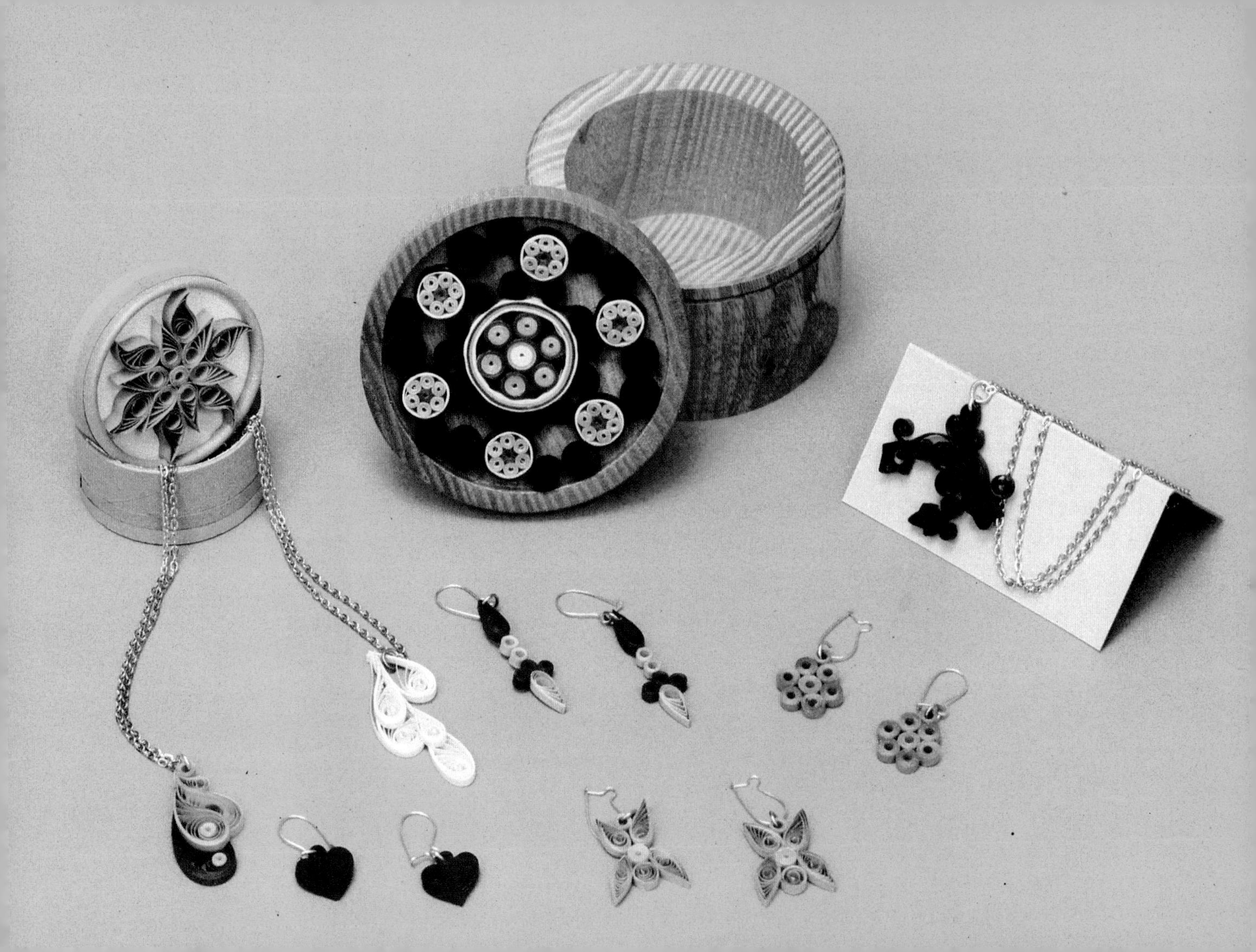

Frames and Borders

Quilled frames for photographs, small pictures etc., are very attractive. It is always a good idea to sketch the frame first, not necessarily to scale e.g. 1. & 2., and then using a grid, make it up to your sketch. Filigree shapes are ideal for this purpose.

The detailed section, 3., is taken from the 17th Century picture illustrated on page 19, it is very ornate and gilded, sloping from the outside down towards the inside.

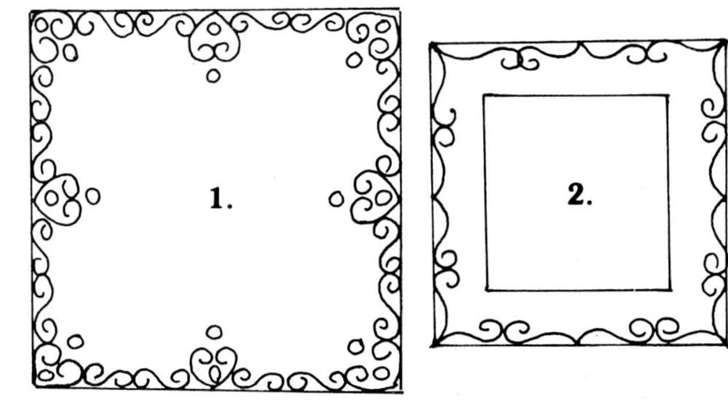

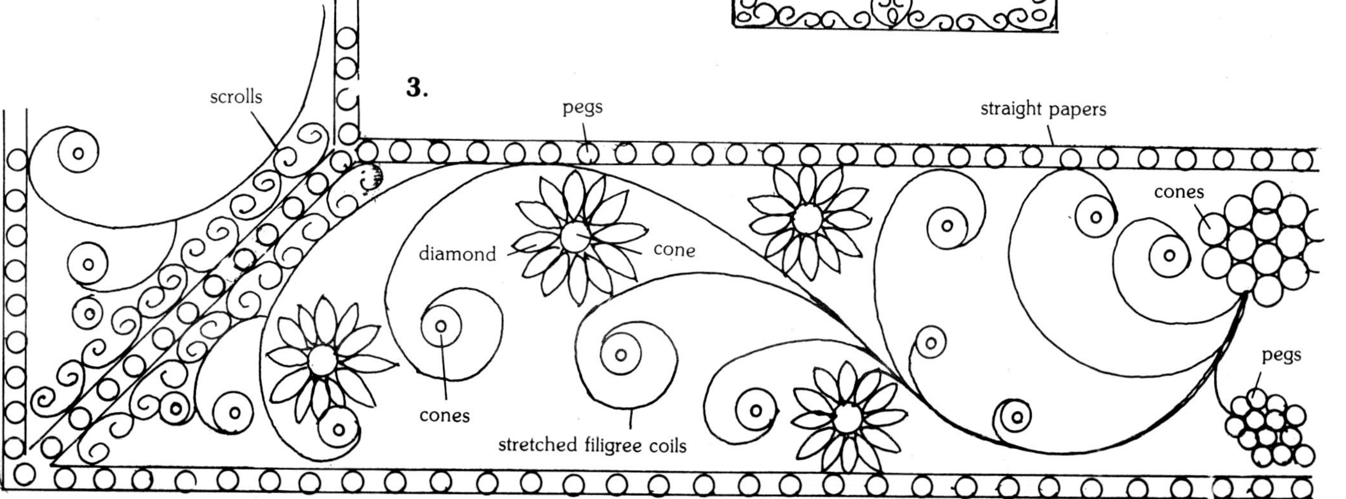

Spring Designs

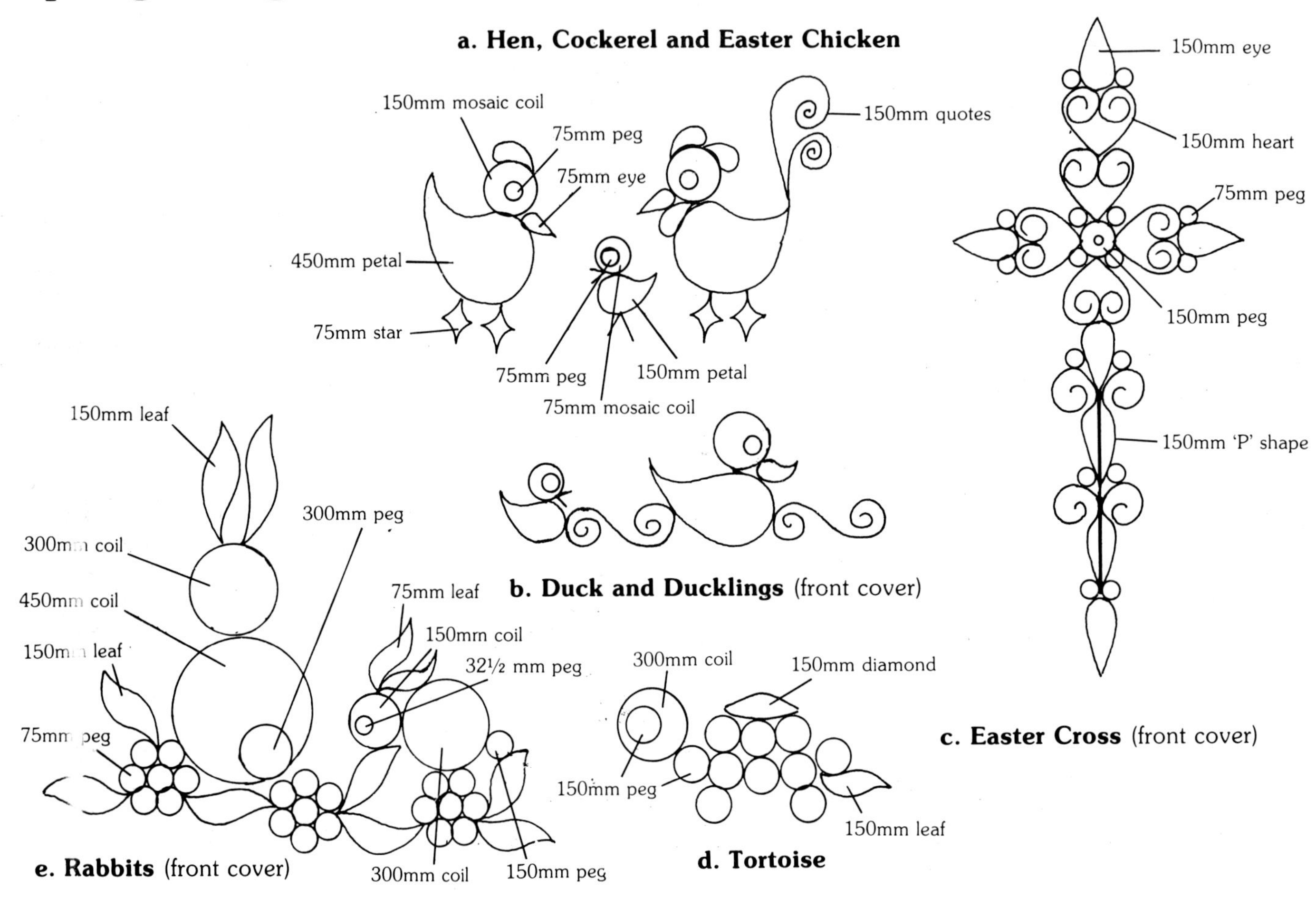

a. **Hen, Cockerel and Easter Chicken**

b. **Duck and Ducklings** (front cover)

c. **Easter Cross** (front cover)

d. **Tortoise**

e. **Rabbits** (front cover)

Note: 1. Details of inserting pegs for eyes on page 10.

2. Details of Gridwork for Easter Cross on page 14.

Spring Designs

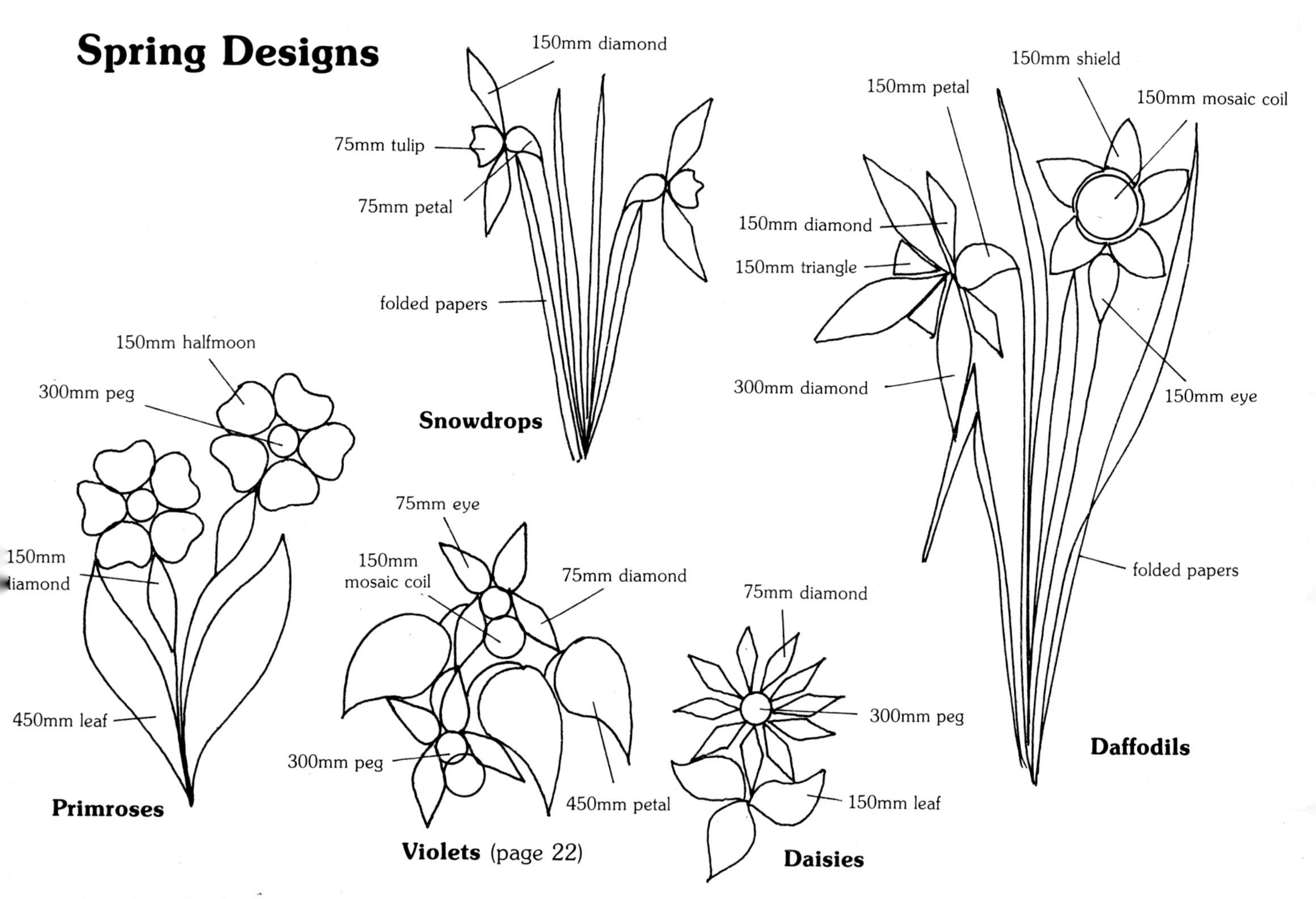

Note: Details of folding papers for leaves on page 10.

Summer Designs

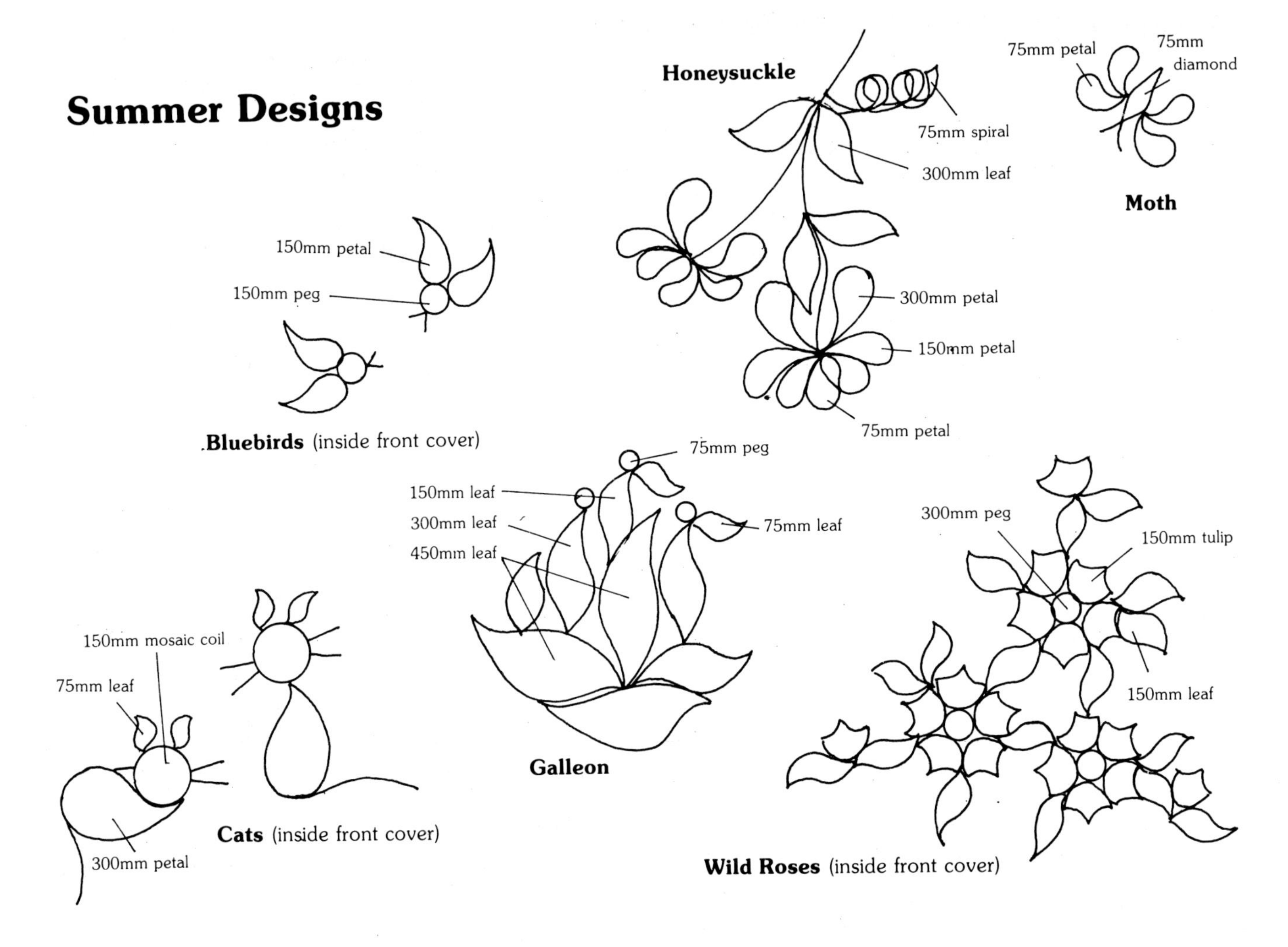

Summer Designs (inside front cover)

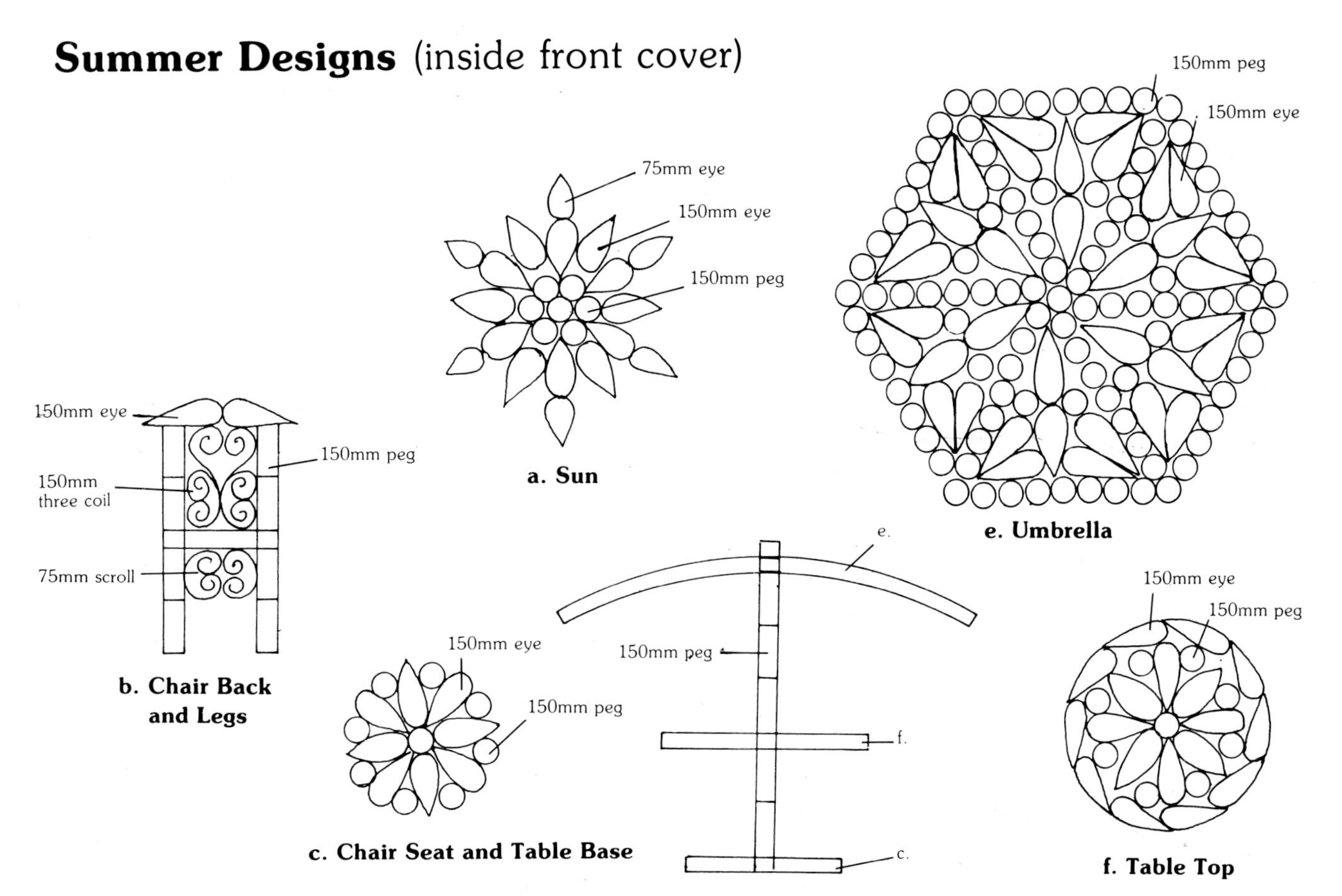

a. Sun

b. Chair Back and Legs

c. Chair Seat and Table Base

d. Cross Section of Table and Umbrella

e. Umbrella

f. Table Top

Note:

1. Details of how to make the table centre and chair legs are on page 13.

2. Details of gridwork on page 14. *3. Details of mouldwork for umbrella on page 18.*

Autumn Designs

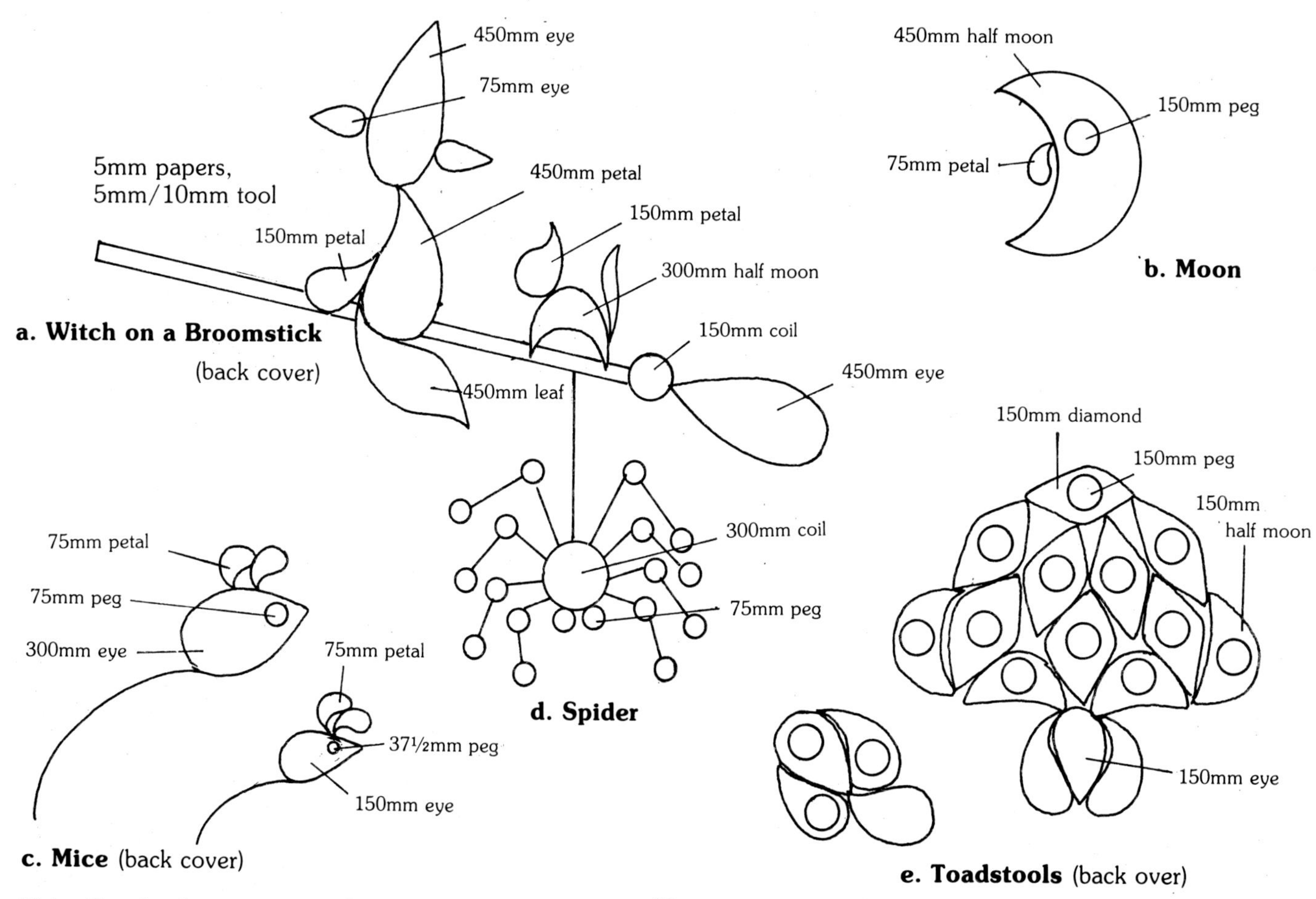

Note: Details of inserting pegs for eyes etc. on page 10.

Autumn Designs

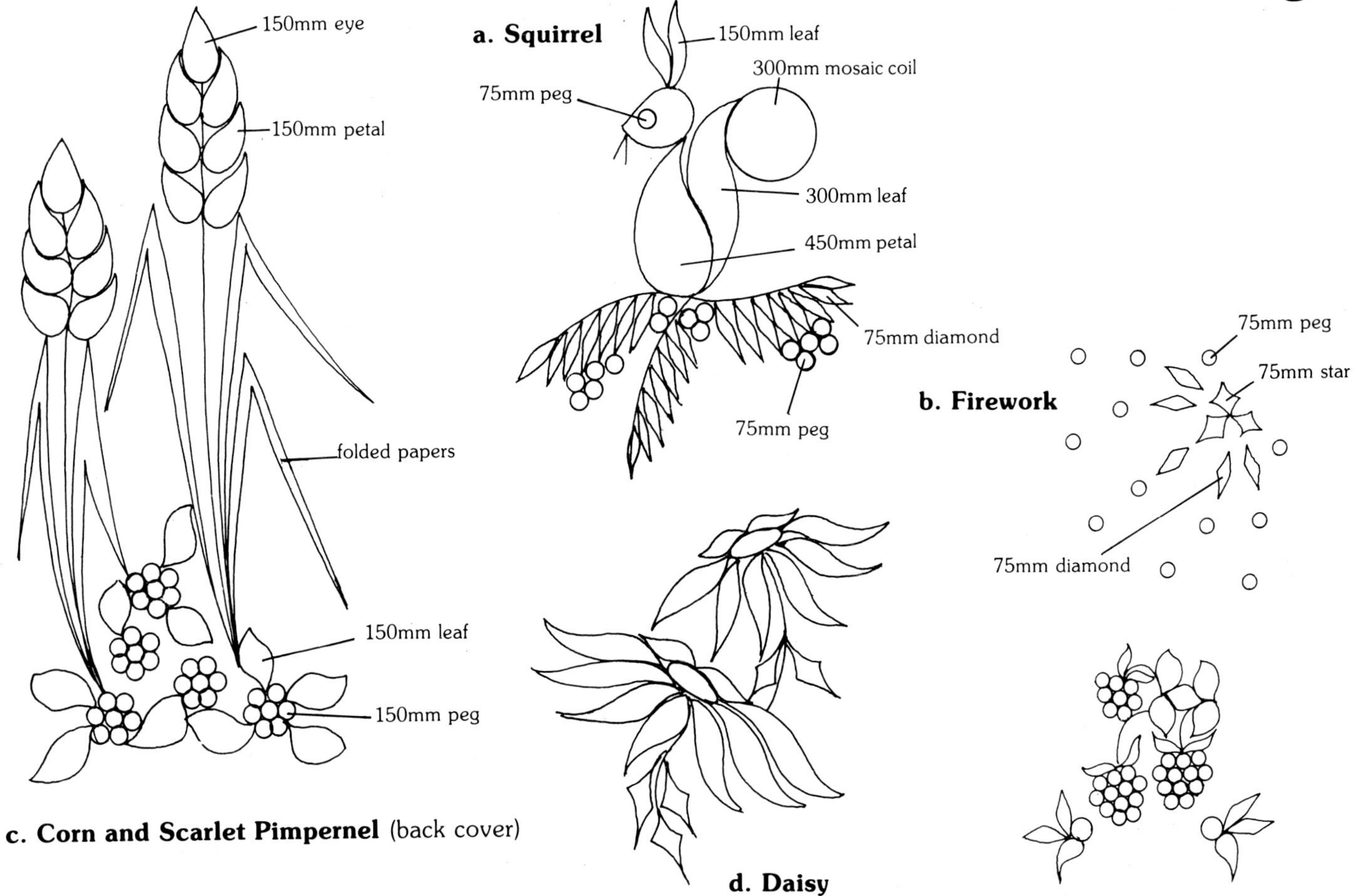

c. **Corn and Scarlet Pimpernel** (back cover)

d. Daisy

e. Blackberries and Bees

Note: 1. Details of inserting pegs for eyes on page 10.
2. Details of folding papers on page 10.

Winter Designs

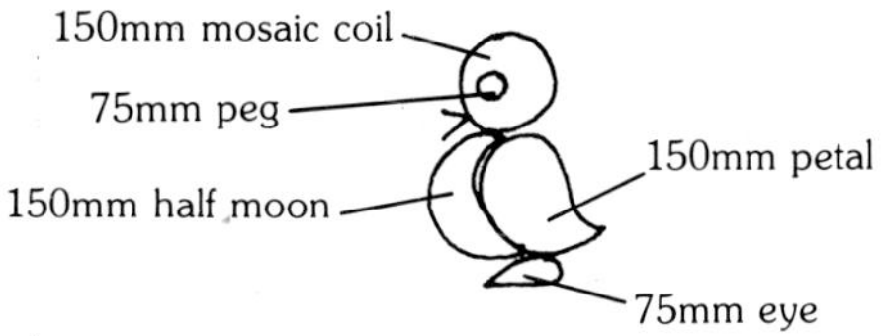

a. Robin (inside back cover)

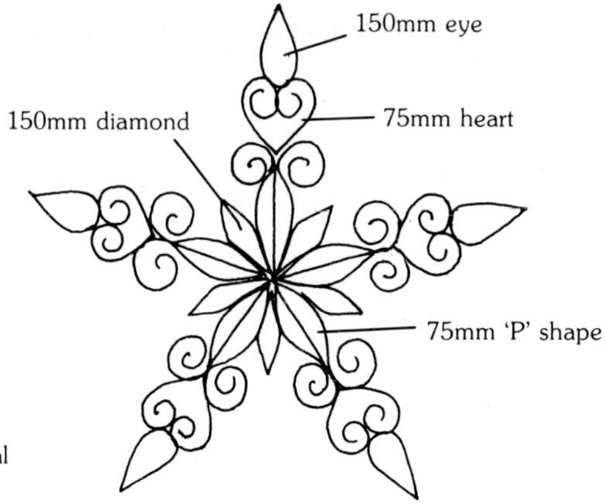

150mm mosaic coil
75mm peg
150mm half moon
150mm petal
75mm eye

150mm eye
75mm heart
150mm diamond
75mm 'P' shape

b. Snowflake

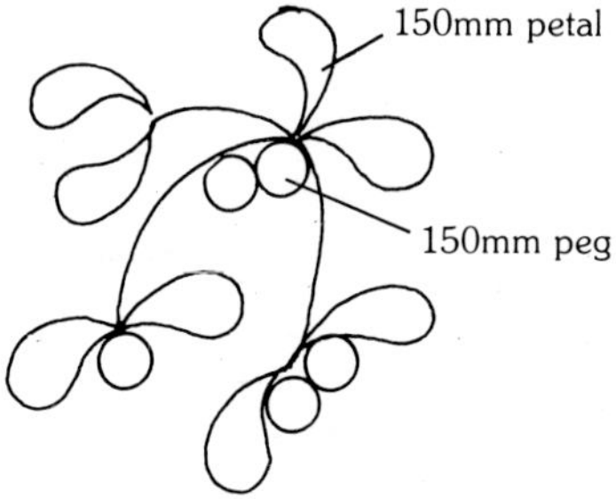

150mm petal
150mm peg

c. Mistletoe

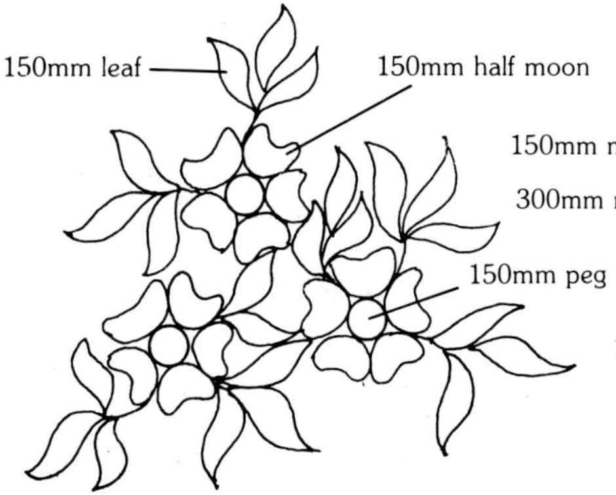

150mm leaf
150mm half moon
150mm peg

d. Christmas Rose (inside back cover)

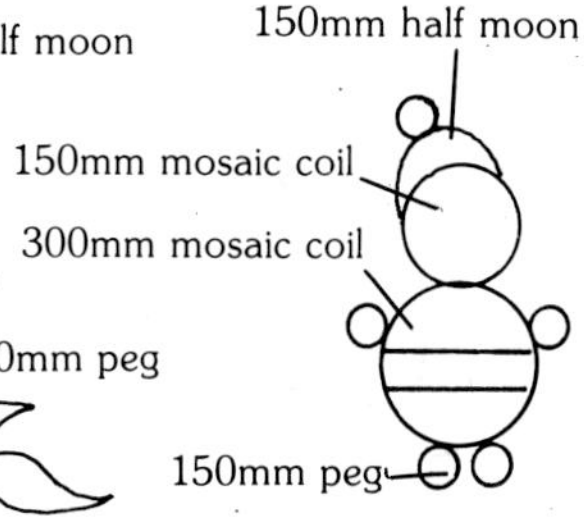

150mm half moon
150mm mosaic coil
300mm mosaic coil
150mm peg

e. Father Christmas

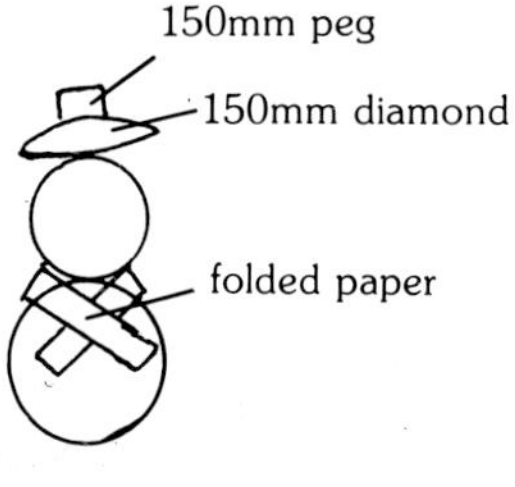

150mm peg
150mm diamond
folded paper

f. Snowman (inside back cover)

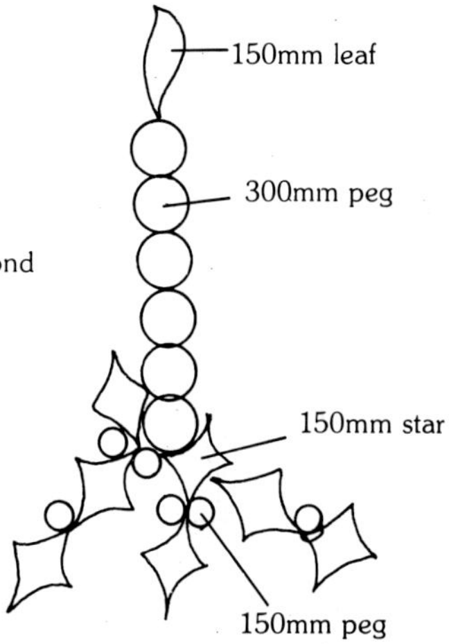

150mm leaf
300mm peg
150mm star
150mm peg

g. Candle and Holly

Note: Details of inserting pegs for eyes on page 10.

Winter Designs (inside back cover)

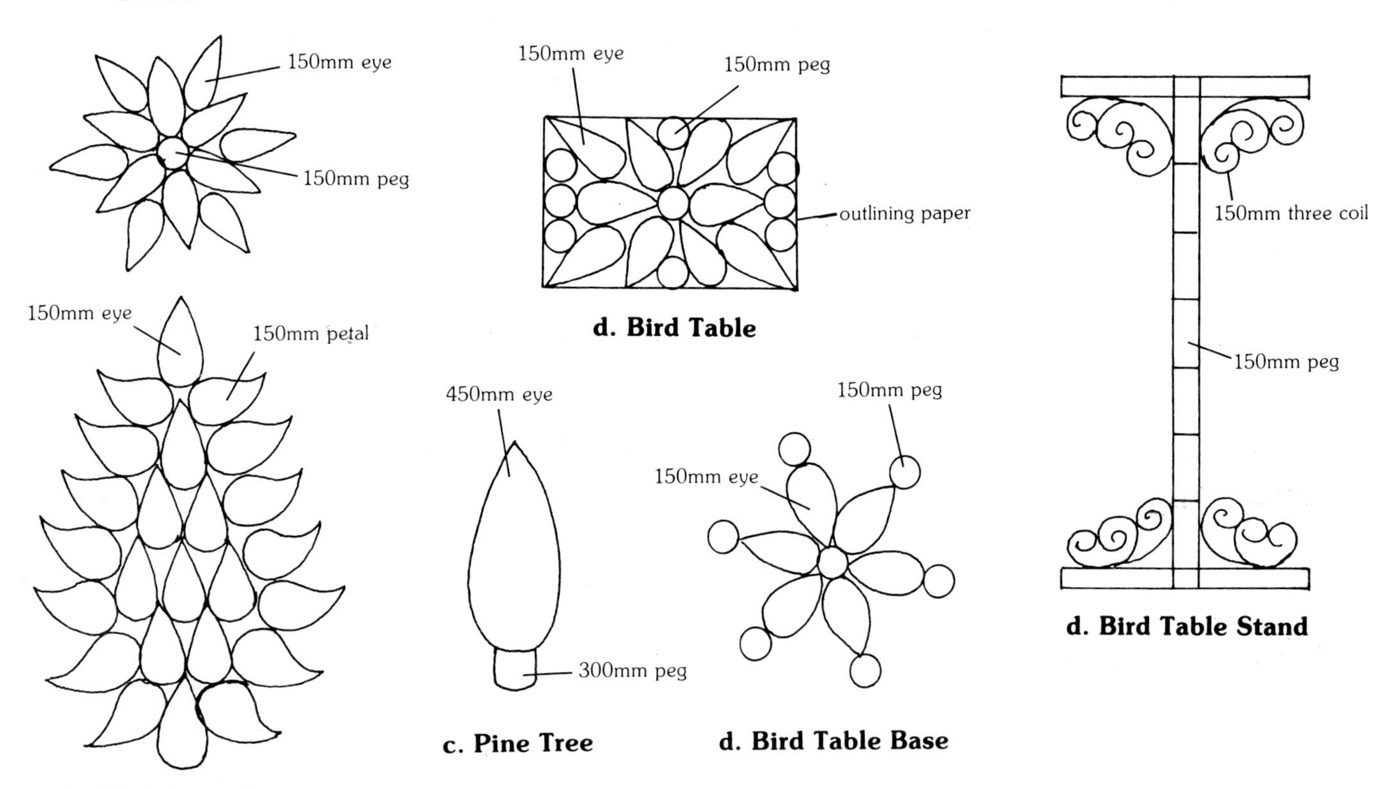

a. Star

b. Christmas Tree

c. Pine Tree

d. Bird Table

d. Bird Table Base

d. Bird Table Stand

Note: 1. Details of gridwork and outlining on page 14.

2. Details of three dimensional work on page 13.

Special Occasion Designs

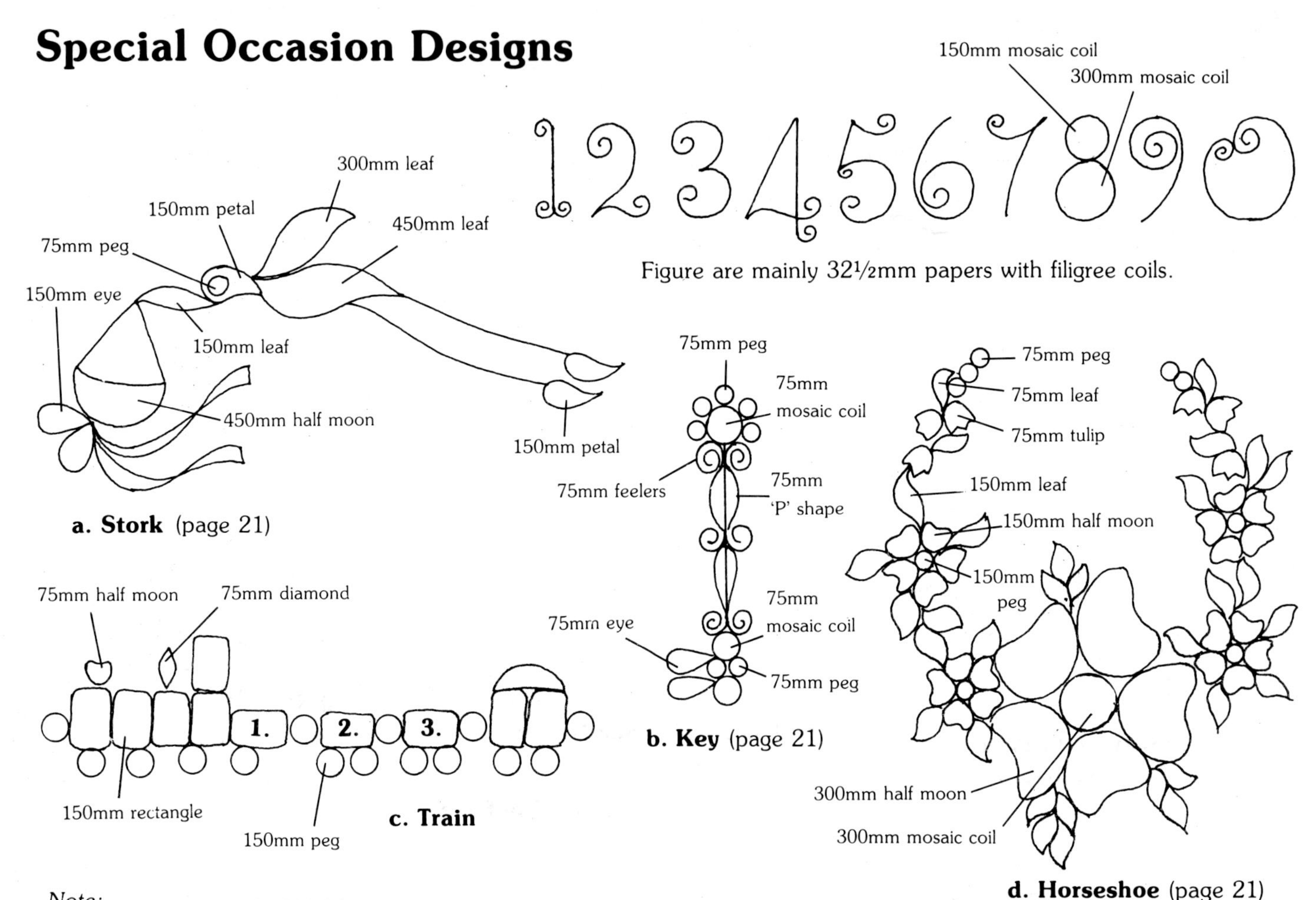

Figure are mainly 32½mm papers with filigree coils.

a. Stork (page 21)

b. Key (page 21)

c. Train

d. Horseshoe (page 21)

Note:

1. Details of inserting pegs for eyes on page 10.

2. Details of gridwork on page 14.

Jewellery and Jewel or Gift Boxes

75mm leaf
75mm three coil
75mm tulip

a. Filigree necklace
(page 22)

150mm leaf
150mm peg
75mm eye
300mm peg
2 colour
300mm eye

b. Owl

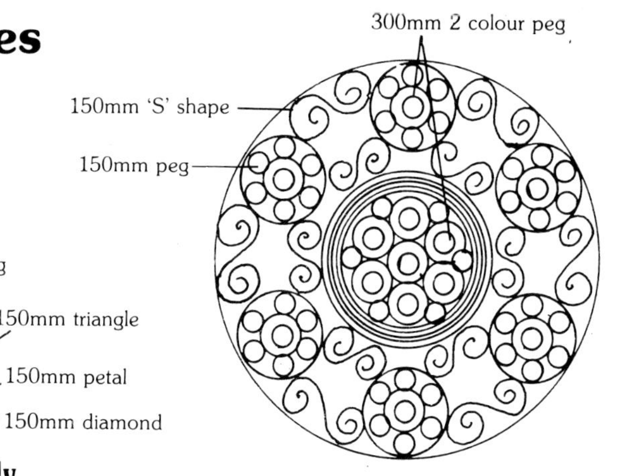

c. Butterfly

d. 18th Century style design for Box Lid (page 22)

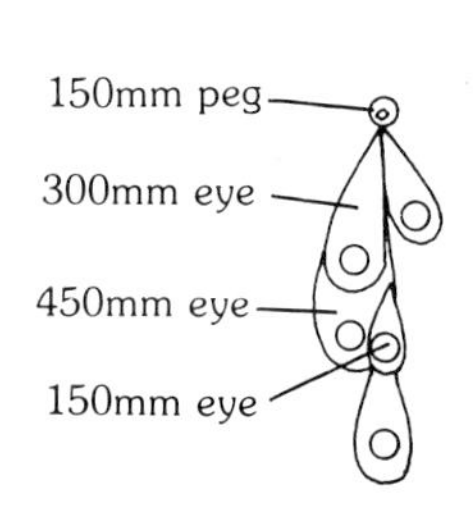

150mm peg
150mm petal
300mm petal
450mm petal

e. Abstract Necklace Designs (page 22)

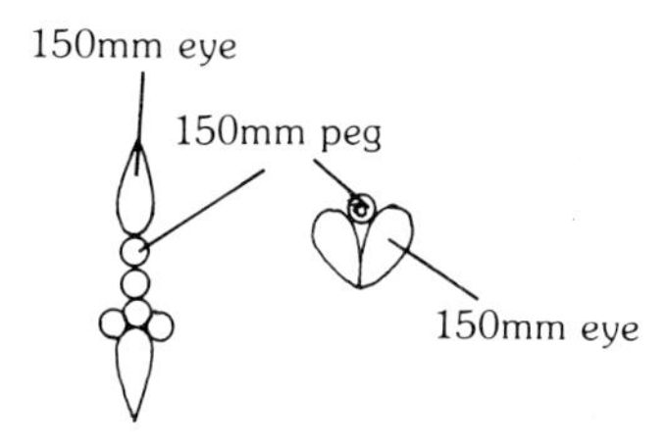

f. Abstract Earring Designs
(page 22)

150mm petal
150mm eye
300mm peg

g. Design for Gift Box Lid
(page 22)

Note:
1. Details of size variation on page 12.
2. Details of two colour shapes on page 10.
3. Details of gridwork on page 14.
4. Details of embellishment on page 15.

Dragon

(page 20)

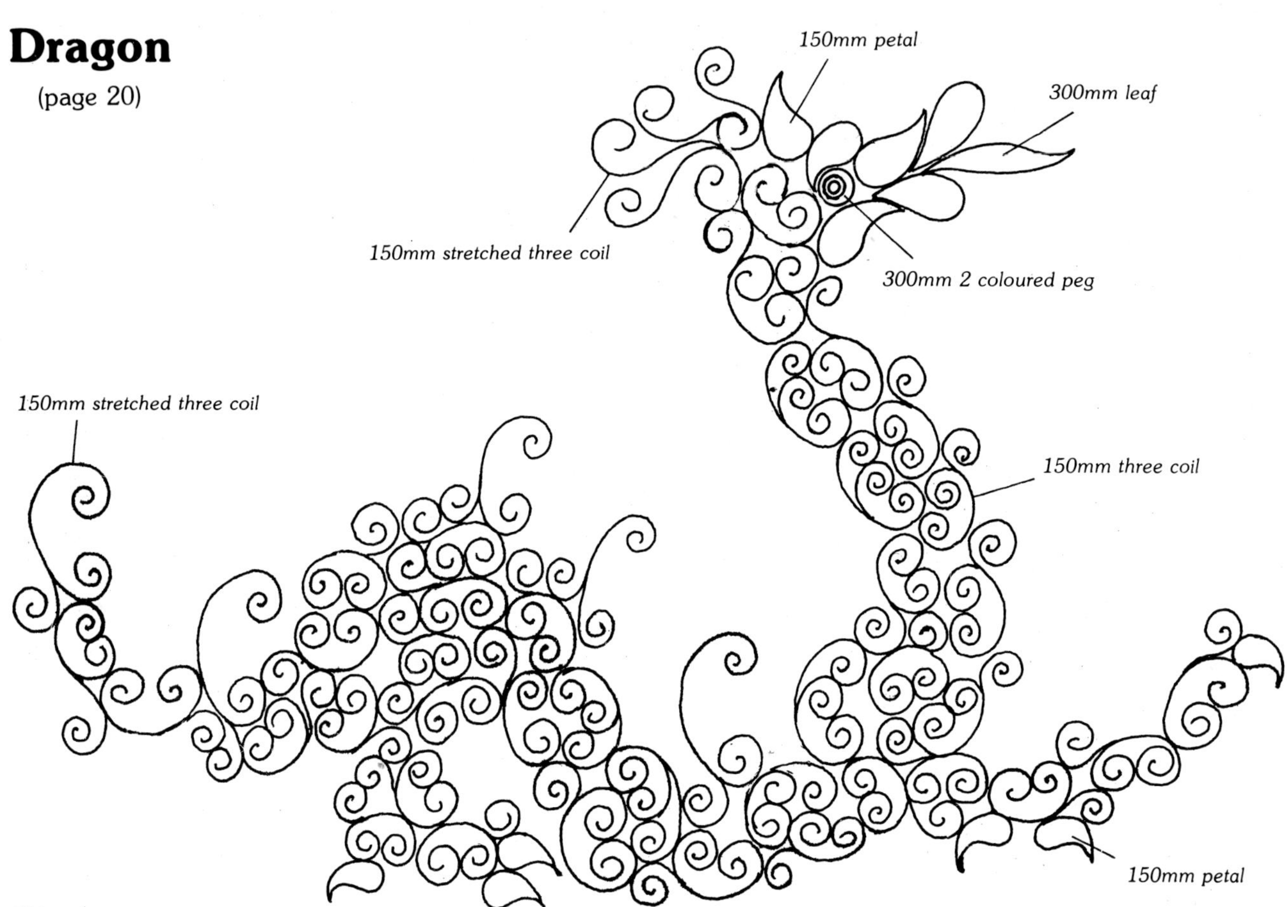

Note:

1. Details of 2 coloured shapes on page 10

Sea Horse

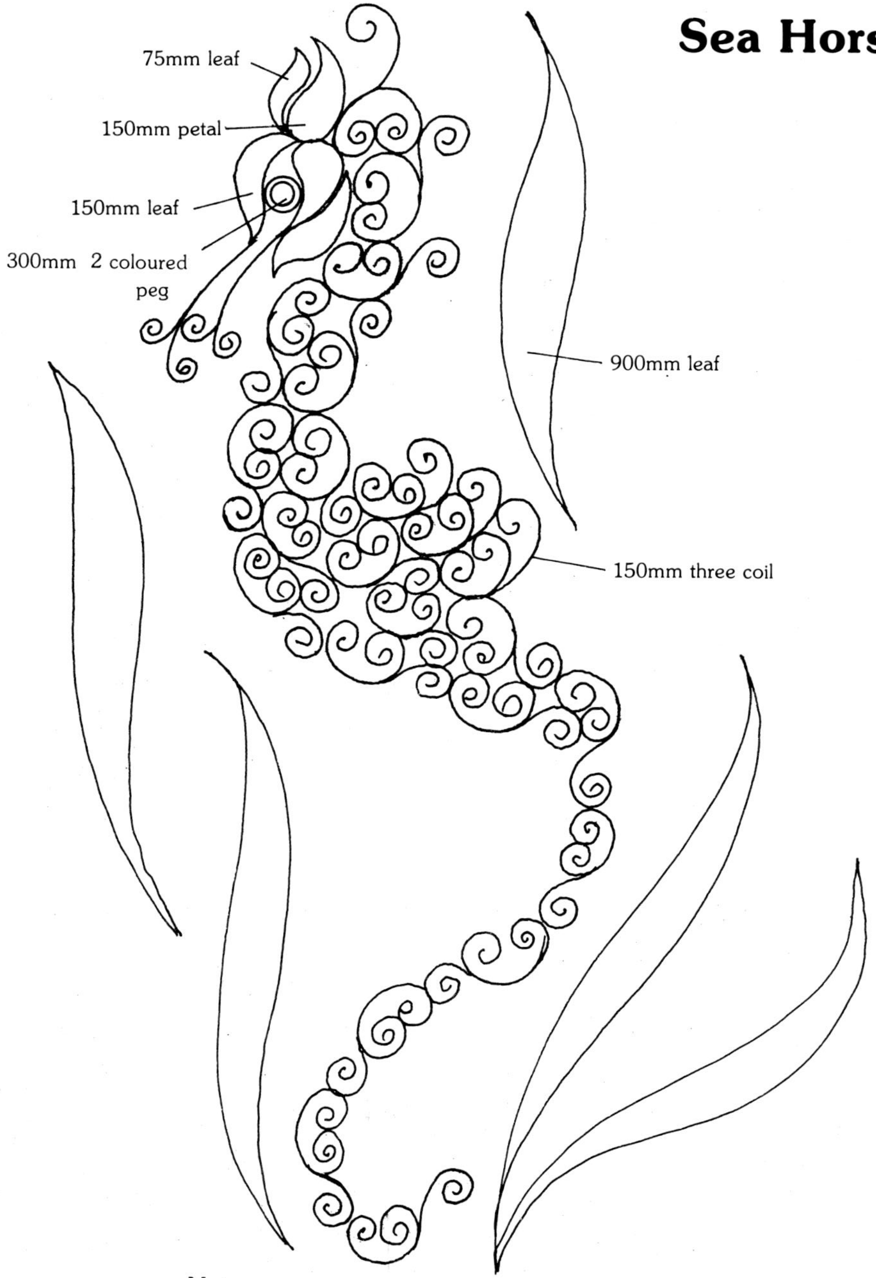

75mm leaf

150mm petal

150mm leaf

300mm 2 coloured peg

900mm leaf

150mm three coil

Note.

1. Details of 2 coloured shapes on page 10.

Quilled Alphabet

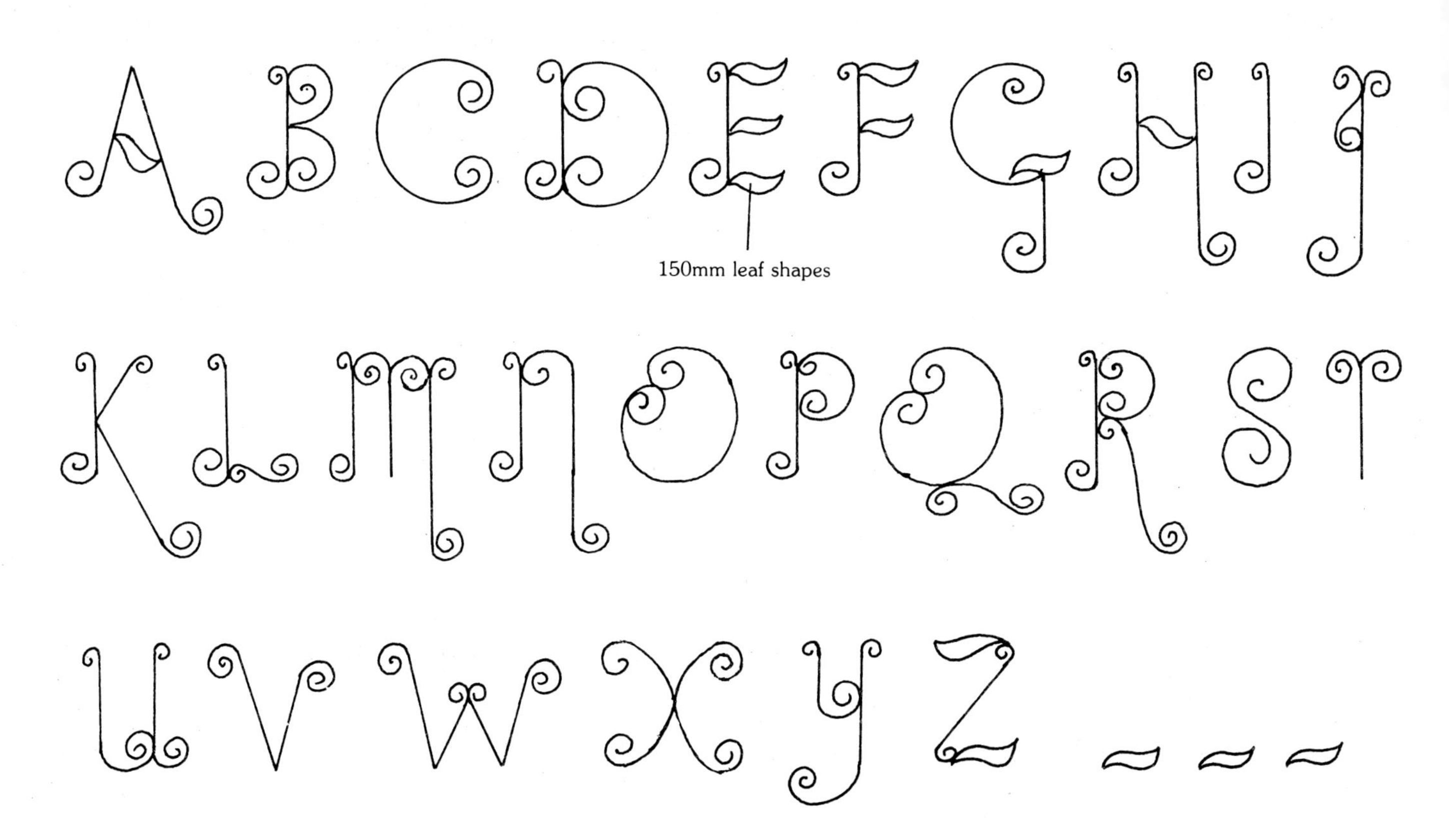

The letters consist mainly of 75mm and 32½mm papers with filigree coils

Mobiles

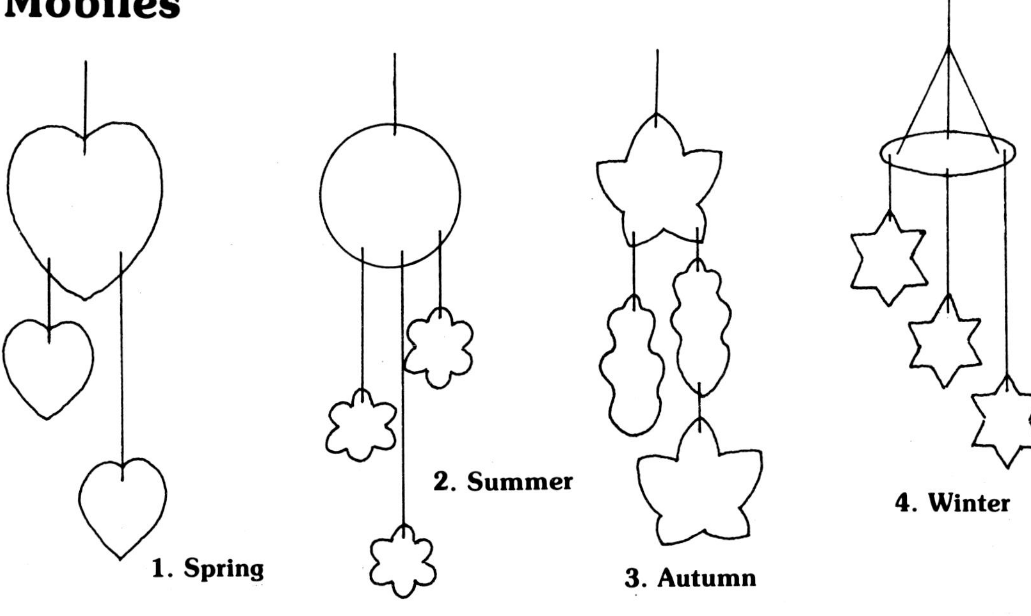

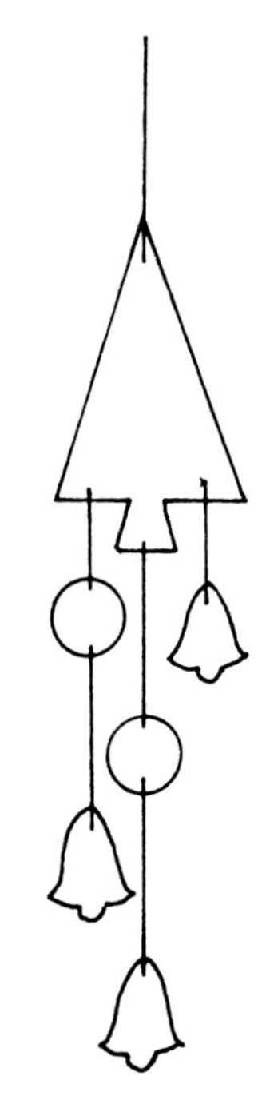

The above ideas are for mobiles using the templates on pages 16 and 17, either as outline guides or background shapes for decorating.

The top template from which the mobiles are hung may be used either in a horizontal or a vertical position.

Transparent nylon sewing thread, or very fine fishing line are suitable for hanging the mobiles.

Three dimensional quilled designs may also be used.

Index

Colour plates

f.c. — front cover
i.f.c. — inside front cover
b.c. — back cover
i.b.c. — inside back cover

Acknowledgements

The Author would like to thank her mother for introducing her to quilling and to her family for their help and patience.

The Author would also like to thank Adrian Heapy Photography, The Butts, Belper, Derby, and the printers, J H Hall & Sons Limited of Derby, for their help and guidance.

Duffield, Derby, 1985

Supplies

Quilling supplies are normally available from good craft shops and craft centres in some departmental stores, in case of difficulty in obtaining them contact:

Past Times, Cumberhills Road, Duffield, Derby DE6 4HA

PAST TIMES